The You That All Along Has Housed You: A Sequence

D0221894

Leslie Ullman

NINE MILE PRESS

The You That All Along Has Housed You: A Sequence

Publisher: Nine Mile Art Corp.
Cover Art: by Dottie Moore, "Khuana."

The publishers gratefully acknowledge support of the New York
State Council on the Arts with the support of Governor Andrew
M. Cuomo and the New York State Legislature. We also
acknowledge support of the County of Onondaga and CNY Arts
through the Tier Three Project Support Grant Program. We have
also received significant support from the Central New York
Community Foundation. This publication would not have been
possible without the generous support of these groups. We are
very grateful to them all.

ISBN-10: 1-7326600-3-4
ISBN-13: 978-1-7326600-3-8

Table of Contents

The You That All Along Has Housed You: A Sequence

A divorce. My friends and I seeking
higher versions of ourselves in sweat-
lodges, hypnosis, and Sufi dancing.
Phyllis, Monica, Kelly, Ken.
Red wine days. Vegetarian days.
Madonna, Michael Jackson, and the noisy
hum of a Kaypro 16 as words flowed
through my fingers, in green, MS-DOS
the new frontier. A 40th birthday —
potluck with margaritas, friends
wandering into the nearby fields
with poems on their breath, and me
held briefly in the glow of new, perfect love.
Kathleen, Sandra, Terri, Renee.
I drove a Toyota Tercel and wore long
beaded earrings. Listened to a Walkman
while riding Burly along the mesa,
picking spines out of my heart
and moving under a shroud of promises
to myself I had broken. One night
I found a rattlesnake in my house.
Hollowed out and ready for re-birth
by the end of the year, I learned to
breathe out angers I could touch
and sorrows I didn't know
had been hiding. The breathing
got deeper. The snake got away.
U-2, Whitney Huston, The Moody Blues.
The breathing was like digging with a sharp
stick. And the peeling away of masks.

Masks

Feathers in the hair. Midnight above
the lashes. Thigh-high boots. Rooms filled
with the shimmer of wind chimes, the anguish
of Coltrane, the water-and-leaf-filtered light of Satie….

I read *The Story of O* and didn't like it
but something made me reach for the chords

it missed. Desire as a black diamond. Not-quite danger.
Sometimes I watched Lawrence Welk for a furtive
return to my mid-century childhood, embalmed as it was

in the syrup of his careful English, the accordions
and bland lyrics—so much smiling
and blondness, innocence tenacious as tar —
I cringed with embarrassment and longing.

My nature made no sense to me.
Nor did the future. I was like everyone I knew.

I preferred foods I couldn't recognize—
bite-sized, jewels scattered on trays
in minimally-furnished salons I could only

imagine—even the hosts dressed in black
and ate standing up. Soft lighting soothed their
bisque walls from which my imagination
withdrew its clutter —I conjured places

where I could imagine starting over.

I Could Imagine Starting Over

in tree-scented air, eyes
cradled between cheekbone
and brow. Luminous as moonstone.
A face in which to start over.
In a dwelling set so far
into a field it almost touched
forest—a place where the mind
might become a canvas. And the hand
its accomplice, offering dried asters
and stones the color of waves, weathered
to translucence, oval, tumbling like coins
from the palm. Once, surrounded by
strangers, I picked up an ostrich egg
and couldn't put it down. I've
been searching ever since
and finding more secrets revealed
through the hand and the tensile surface of eye—
the eye so in need of protection
but taking in the world.
The whole thing at once.

Taking In The World. The Whole Thing At Once.

This is what parents tell their offspring
not to do, viewing a child's greed
as the mirror they must turn to the wall.
Don't reach…. You're not entitled….
But taking in, receiving, the brought-up self
backing off and leaving a wondering,
porous self—eyes, ears, nose, taste buds
like sea creatures swaying under water—
this is appetite that honors. And asks nothing.
Narcissism is the hole hollowed true
black, self's need usurping others'
air and the light in their minds
and getting away with it. A blindness
to so much that gathers around us
whether or not we notice. I could give up
the *me* that curls like a slug
with salt thrown over it when someone
sucks all the air from the room
but not the noticing.

The Noticing

holds things in place
the way roofs clamp walls
to floors and corners, and trees
send invisible branches deep
into earth, steadying
the commotion of wind.

The noticing tosses the jacket
on the back of a chair.
Smooths it over the narrow ridge
of the present. Replays
the chair's first coat of varnish
and the jockeying of legs
and seat through the doorway.

Every bike lying on its side, every
plastic ball or block left on the lawn
was last touched by a child's hand
before the call to come inside—a hand
sticky with juice, or gritty from digging
a hole through the garden towards China.

Bouquet of spoons and spatulas in a jug,
papers stacked and weighted with a smoky
river stone—smooth, fist-sized—beside three pens
and a postcard from Morocco, clamshell
full of sea glass—all these still-lives left
by the hand in its gatherings and settings-down,
each one a moment. Each one a world.

Each One A World

If you behold some paintings long enough
you can, for example, smell the snow
in Sisley's Louveciennes at twilight.
Or feel the ennui of Picasso's pale woman
looking away from the man across the table.

The shoulder of a demi-nude, carried
home on a Renoir postcard, can warm the skin
of the living palm. Light becomes liquid, pouring
Vermeer's noon from a window
onto a woman pouring milk from a pitcher

or pools from a Van Gogh streetlamp—
brandy, honey, gold, the miracle
of spark and heat discovered
by mistake long ago
when two pieces of flint

fell from someone's hands and
struck against one another, igniting
twig and leaf in the dark
world that had held
its breath, waiting for this moment.

Waiting For This Moment

the cooking fire
lit the oil lamp
into light-switch into
neon glare into fiber optics,
real time and weather disguised
layer by layer as man sought
protection for his peltless skin,
his eye that dimmed at twilight
and his helpless, swaddled young.

Dots, pools, densities of light
spilled over the land into a vastness
filled with dangers living mostly
inside the human brain folded
over and in on itself
like a tropical flower

from which a Babel of tongues flew across
ocean and landmass, compressed
and driven through cables,
while the earth beneath
continued shifting
plate by plate
in its slow
dealings with drought
and flood, thaw and freeze,
tasting time the way time
was meant to be tasted.

Time, Tasted

Run through the fingers.
Stroked like the ears of a loved animal.
Taken by surprise.
Being taken as surprise.
Divided into days
and made into foundation and walls.
Forgotten inside the right-hand chambers
of the brain when the hand dances with clay.
Wet when the hand dances with clay
and smeared with streaks when colors
run together on a palette. Stitched
into seams, lost in a book, absorbed by
a poem. Hard to waste.

Waste?

As if lamentation had never
been tried before, I sit at a keyboard
and reach for words—as if bearing witness
to the ten-hour assembly line, the nation's
clogged veins of commerce, and
the absence of soul in elected officials
might excuse me from the tribe.

I've never missed a meal except by choice.
Have never watched a loved-one obliterated
or lost roof and walls and everything inside them.
Have never been taken, never been bound
and only sometimes find myself in the path
of nature with its gloves off, my mettle
gathering mostly in imagination.

Perhaps a soldier with half my schooling
could teach me what it means to rush into smoke
and blind corners with only my wits and my rage.
Rage that finds its way from heart to sinew.
Courage that doesn't give itself a name. What
would I rise to? Relinquish? Untested, I melt down
tired words and reshape them. Still in the dark.

In The Dark

Wasn't it just yesterday that Christmas
and birthdays took forever to arrive? That items
with an on/off switch were fed from a heart
of fuses inside the house, or from batteries
possessed of a single life?—phonograph, radio,
flashlight under the covers, transistor
on the beach, percolator, black & white TV,

then the IBM Selectric that pulled words
fast through the fingers. My first computer
weighed thirty-five pounds and hummed,
all circuits a mantra—I found myself
writing things moments before
I knew what I was saying.

Now everything I rely on
has to be re-charged every night.

And when the flight attendant asks us,
in preparation for take-off, to power down
any device that speaks with another device
I'm suddenly lost in my seat, spinning towards
panic. Or boredom. Returned to a vastness
that's been waiting all along inside
my mind, that ersatz boundary.

Ersatz Boundaries

Dawn in the Northeast, a single
bird trilling New England bird-sounds
while I'm afraid to go back to sleep
and miss the plane west. Off the green
New York Thruway into the twilight-
zone of airports, non-hub to non-hub, three
flights, a whole expensive day
suspended, levelled, reconstituted
into something I no longer recognize,
just as I no longer inhabit a body
that would never ask for a Diet Coke.
Escape-reading. Standing in line. The carry-on
gaining weight. A fat breathless person
in the next seat into the Central Time Zone
but then, into Mountain Time, a tiny girl-child
with a Buddha face, taking all of me
into the gentle pool of a gaze I carry with me
into the shuttle, into my car, into the deepening
light of late afternoon, into the rock and sage
of the mountains, the last and longest part
of the day also the gentlest. Already my body
forgets the laws of time and gravity
it has spent a day breaking. Soon it will
again take for granted the freedom
to go outside and feel grass underfoot
still damp from the sprinkler
and come back inside only when night
sets in with the chill that announces
it has truly arrived.

When Night Announces It Has Truly Arrived

a seam of tension unstitches itself
and I am no longer dangling
from a hook over what I owe
or haven't finished. The future
recedes, letting me drift into a feeling
like watercolor and cool sheets. Cat
leaning into my hip. The book I've postponed
inviting me where all day I've wished
to be going—perhaps a village where stories
pass themselves around a fire, and children
weave among them, outside the glare of fortune
and shallow history. Some evenings I can
almost taste another life, as if carrying water
from a stream gave heft to my day. Gathering wood.
Reading at leisure the light changing angles through
trees, the approach of a storm, and fire-lit faces
I knew as well as my own. Tapping a frequency
that settled me, yes, into sleep. And then into waking.

And Then Into Waking

When the rising sun
washes everything clean,
all shadows fresh and sharp
and the sky a rested magenta, it touches
one by one the houses in Lower las Colonias,
the patchwork of fields, the trucks
in their driveways still parked
and gleaming after night, too, has
washed them down. Contours and colors
pop. This is how sagebrush looked to me
after new lenses had been pressed and sealed
into my nearsighted eyes—I saw
its textures all the way to the horizon.
Such clarity lifted me into a realm
of expectation. As though light itself
were currency that could be exchanged for
the one thing I didn't know I needed.
So this, I thought, is how dawn feels to
the land it watches over, as I drove
three hours to an early plane at a time
when I usually arise behind blinds,
already burdened by the day to come.

The Day To Come

is best left to its own trajectory. *Why not*
live in the moment? Today I parked my bike
against someone's adobe wall, beside
an acequia, and sat drinking water
and watching water flow from snowmelt
four thousand feet up. That liquid, muscled
sound—I stopped the day to stay in its
mantra—the ripples bursting joyous
from corrugated pipe into the wider ditch,
the dance of sunlight on slippery green,
the feeling of being held there, something gritty
sluiced away, residue of my father's passing.
For a while that month I had lost my voice, my throat
a dried river. The ashes I brought home
surprised me. Heavy. I'll scatter them
this winter, on his favorite trail, then let snowmelt
gather and guide them where water knows to go.

Where Water Knows To Go

First it loosens its ice-fists, and rime
from spruce limbs, and crystal
lace from windows—they shine
in surrender, at the border where
sun keeps at last the promise
it withheld all winter. What froze
trembles, then turns to ghost-
shapes which then acquiesce to
two kinds of *down*—into ground
and over ground, along with ashes
scattered according to some last wishes
from the top of Kachina Peak,
around swells and rocks into roots,
arroyos, Rio Pueblo, Rio Hondo,
hoarded and played in and fought over....
Alfalfa and cotton on either side of
the Rio Grande—I can see from a plane
their green swathe across the desert,
ashes and old snow and the frost
that made my gloves stick to metal
gleaming in that green, feeding that green.
And then? What does water touch
when heat lifts it into cloud and jet stream
where it only *seems* to disappear
and from which it may
or may not return?

Re-turn

can mean to turn again. Or
make the same turn twice.
Or trace a spiral that moves
at once inward and outward—you can
bend your attention either way.
Both directions appear improbably
at once, the way an Escher print
shows water flowing seamlessly
upward and down. Don't ask,
just let something like vertigo
wash over you, quelling
whatever you knew of time or logic
until sensation is all.

Something of a drugged state.
And sometimes it's your past that
circles back in waves to converse
with your present. A slow dance
with partners you discover you can trust—
no great loves, no awkward groping or
sweaty palms, each old heartbreak
now blunt-edged and forgettable.
You've been around this block.
And perhaps are moving closer to the *you*
that all along has housed you.

The You That All Along Has Housed You

was once a Druid, an unwed mother, a teller of
white lies, and a friar's apprentice; prefers movement
to meditation, altitude to ocean; has no tolerance
for overhead lighting but is drawn like a crow
to glittery things—also to spiral-shaped things—
can read people like tea leaves but can't find
the scissors or the milk or clean socks even when
they're in plain sight; was once a painter inside
a cave, and a healer slipping quiet as a spider from
a wooden hut at dawn; knows how to work leather
and name the gemstones; knows that a teak bowl
is not the right vessel for holding coins; grew angry at God
lifetimes ago—heartbroken—died broken—and now
gropes its way life after life towards a light it still can't define.

spills gold, butter, something honeyed
from strangers' windows at night. A promise
that can't be defined but inexplicably
consoles and uplifts, hinting at
book opened on a table, nest of chair,
heat purring through vents, repose.
So someone who's been on a train all day
and moving too fast might borrow a flash of
a stranger's evening, something commonplace
as the flick of a switch. Memory kindled
along with trace wonder early men and women
must have felt when they trial-and-erred
in the shelter of caves, a piece of flint
in each hand, and history heaved itself towards
a new threshold. Cooked meat. Tools.
The dulled edge of winter. Protection
from animals whose jeweled eyes—
perhaps deadly, perhaps inquisitive—
glowed restless in the shadows.

Inquisitive In The Shadows

I used to crouch in a special hollow inside
the neighbors' hedge after dark
playing hide-and-seek, the hide
more compelling than the seek.
The hedge turned me into a piece
of night. An invisible force
surveying pools of light from lampposts
and windows, the freshly tarred street
a wash of black from which I'd slipped
unseen. Such sweetness in being shrouded
in friendly leaves, in the Midwest
those short nights of summer,
dogs and children running free
through velvet darkness and the scent
of blossoms none of us
could name. A perfume
that held out a promise, a question,
an elegance we might grow into
but not yet. Cricket song wove among
the shadows, vibration of a future
which, not yet a doorway
opening to accomplishment
or bright rooms, waited in the distance,
benign and indistinct, a dim shape under the stars.

A single dream sometimes follows me, in
fragments, through waves of my sleep.
A bone that worries the night
and leaves no trace. A half-story
nosing its way, blind, through seams
that almost block its flow. And I
follow, tethered and unresisting—
where does it come from and who
is the dreamer? I might as well be
a mountain—dark, inert, but teeming
with burrowing animals and restless
leaves—an ecosystem littered with
something overheard, a chanced-upon
photo, a friend's distress, an obsession
over luggage that gets left behind
only in my sleep—such nights
require work that never gets finished.
A recycling of detritus through soil
unsure of which roots to nourish,
which roots to let wither underground

Underground

Imperceptibly, three times a week, my
twitchy mind learns to drop into the stretch,
twist, reach, breath of yoga and almost
disappears—or at least floats alongside
the body, humming but muted,
a ghost-mind—while the body
feels gravity as seduction and ballast,
feels at once vast and dense, porous
and path-wayed, feels breath and warmth
moving through organs, veins, and cilia hitherto
unacknowledged, like whatever goes on
beneath the mulch of my garden each year
to brighten summer perennials and then
keep them, through winter's long sear
and subtraction, supple and
resting in secret.

Secrets

Someone has vacated the premises,
the one who digs in the dark and comes back
with gold. The others mind the store
and have no truck with mysteries

that breathe out there beyond
the straightforward fluorescents,
the predictable clock, the coins
exchanged for dry goods. I beseech

this someone for whom doors swing both
ways, on easy hinges, and whose intermittent
presence is more aura than conversation
but translates into word-strings lit

with journeys: *Come home, come home, help me
clear a path to the smoky fires and gypsy
songs, the questions that made me answer
in tongues. Come home and replenish the vein*

and sometimes a string of notes wafts
from beyond what the ear knows, or a scent
from vanished worlds, or a scrap of memory
not mine that leads to a scene I can feel

and describe but don't—it's all
translation. My bones stretch, then
dissolve. I reach for stars. For a time
I believe I can touch them.

For A Time I Believe I Can Touch Them

when silence and the absence
of ambient light conspire to remove
all interference between me
and the stars. It helps if moisture
too, is absent, its molecule-chains
condensed or broken apart,
no longer weighing down the lighter
element, air, or blurring the scrim
of night itself. Once I saw the whole
of a new moon, as though my eyes
could touch the rest of what held aloft
that eyelash of light—as though
my eyes were hands restoring
the whole vast shadowed sphere,
adoring. It was midwinter
in Vermont and minus-seventeen,
the air all clench and crystal, the cold
having subtracted everything. Just me
and the moon, held in an arctic fist, our
dark sides showing themselves each to each,
me tired and a little tipsy, the moon
perhaps wanting to share with *something*
a part of itself long invisible and untouched.
And *I* happened to be there. Touched
too, in my own invisible places, which
are many, and were consoled.

Invisible Places, Which Are Many

release breath from the past
when light lengthens and lingers
around them—the space behind books
on mahogany shelves, cobwebbed
corners behind sofas, undersides
of roll-top desks and secret drawers
that sheltered keys, empty drawers
in dressers that once held a froth
of *décor*: lace, jet, snuffbox, linen,
smelling-salt, lavender, cameo, pearl....
Also dust, flakes of varnish,
the vanished hands that once fluttered
or swept them clean of spilled powder
and spider web. Nights of rain tapping
leaded glass. April sun drawing the children out,
their winter skin white and untouched
and oh, that first lick of summer-to-come—
a flush rising up the neck, and green shoots
daring at last to show themselves above
the locked ground. Watercress beckoning
from the frigid stream. The sun growing
strong, sure, sending flame into
all that has been folded in on itself.

Folded In On Itself

Two antennae finger the sunlit air
hesitating, nearly blind, through moisture
and shades of light, towards the promise
of something green. Such risk
to the soft body made mostly of water
but for the durable house it carries
everywhere—it can wind itself back, any time,
and there reside in a perfect architecture,
labyrinth of chambers curving inward, its legacy
left in millennia of sand, water, and stone.
Ammonite. Nautilus. Common snail. Maker
of proportioned chambers measured by instinct
and uplifting. The Parthenon. Cathedrals
plotting the progress of faith through Europe—
did mankind know exactly why this pleased
the eye? Sunflower, ram's horn and fiddlehead fern,
God's eye replaying the world in Its image: spiral.

God's Eye, A Spiral

God's ire, too…. Think, how
anger feeds the coals of itself
into explosion, and hurricanes
gather heft, circling, ripping
roofs and shutters, breaking glass,
and tornadoes pull dense objects
like cars and cattle into a corkscrew
towards—what—heaven?
Spiral. Out of control. Or
dead earnest, bent on
its own velocity, its own
Fibonacci progress, snail's work
magnified thousands-fold. If we took
man's slow push towards upright walking,
fire, tools, electricity, the microscope,
the split atom and pierced sound barrier
and played it fast-forward, we might
see a perfect storm, the world
whirling its way towards its end.

Whirling Its Way Towards Its End

I suspect neither the earth nor mankind are in
immediate peril, as some predict, though I
wouldn't be surprised if we don't have a few
humbling millennia ahead of us once we've made
a hash of things, a hash we haven't
yet foreseen, a hash that may well render us
speechless and forced to live without
the clutter to which we're accustomed.
Meanwhile, there are planes to be caught
and luggage to be lost and reclaimed
and appointments to be kept and loved ones
to be loved better, not to mention a patience
beneath our feet that still offers grassy acres,
wildflowers, gifts of snowmelt, unclimbable
mountains, and the bay horse that galloped today
along a fence line beside the road,
following, as I drove away from home.

As I Drove Away From Home

I resolved not to forget the open acres, their
never-still grasses and sage showing light
green undersides in the wind, adobe
houses hand-smoothed and in want of
sealing and new paint, the Sangre de Christo
wall of pushed-up tectonics, and Pedernale
in the distance—that mystery, that lone
perfect mesa, that monument to
Georgia O'Keeffe who also flourished
alone, towering, in thin air and strong sun—
all this, mine and not mine. My hands
have never scooped the mud that every spring
fills winter's cracks in the venerable church
of St. Francis. The people who've spoken
Spanish here for four centuries, cloistered
and simmering, would never understand
my careful, grammatical attempts, nor I
their guttural remnants of what once was
perfect Castilian. They do not meet
my eye. They count their money slowly
in Walmart's checkout line, as though today's
currency were a foreign language. And I
am a currency even more baffling, barely
tolerated, another degree of pollution in a history
long compromised and made toxic. Culpable
in my birthplace far from this land of *penitentes*
and their *moradas* so old, so earthen, so saturated
in violent and sustaining ritual, they vibrate
behind their locked gates. Yet the land stretches
before all of us day after day, in all shades
of light, unscrolling the gift of itself without holding back.

Not Holding Back

What is required?—a sail
full-belled in the wind. Hand
calm at the helm. Eye trained on
a vague horizon as the harbor
shrinks behind—safe and known
and too small, suddenly, to contain
the future. The vessel's a sturdy
beetle riding the swells. Which grow.
And the depths swell beneath it,
the invisible realm of sand—restless
waves of it—and coral ridges and
caves, seaweeds, fish drifting
in clouds that hold their own light.
Such a universe—feel the vastness
and pull of it, the muscular
power. Go with it. Let guesswork
guide you through all you can't
see. The sky goes with you.
It will answer when you ask.

When You Ask

what will you ask first?
So many choices. And so much
you don't have, though only rarely
is there not enough. Do you remember
wanting something just because
it was a word you didn't know?
Perhaps, it was *hollyhock*.
Long ago. Now there are
words that don't
do enough. *Filibuster*
sounds solid on the tongue,
in the news, but it doesn't hold
when the self you're trying
to come to terms with resists
yet again a pattern whose precursor
is surrender. *Surrender*
has promise. But sometimes withholds
earnest money. Still looks for
the better deal, the dream house,
retribution waiting on the doorstep
and a shape-shifting fulfillment
you never, in spite of yourself,
stopped reaching for, only to
find yourself clutching air. *Fulfillment*....
It's time to outgrow a word
so empty in its clothes—maybe you meant
success. Maybe you meant
being seen. Maybe you meant...
living in another skin next time around.

Next Time Around

I will master the pirouette and the splits
before the age of six (in this life it was
the headstand). Or learn to type
before I can write. Or climb from
my first glimpse of a river
bearing a clay jar of water on my head,
my head proud on its stalk, the water
supple, alive in its enclosure.
I might hear an ancient song rising
unbidden in my throat. Or play
a small stringed instrument while perched
in a tree. Beside the river. Singing
with the river in its own language,
having stepped without
looking back into the life
I've been given, in a country
whose small change flows through
my hands and whose ways are the air
I breathe without knowing I breathe.
I will not have to be taught to dance.
I will feel easy with beasts or, elsewhere
altogether, with the circuits inside
slender electronic devices
and the invisible chambers of the gigabyte.
For a long time I will have few
regrets, alive in that time and place
until my voice, my limbs, my thoughts
begin to reach, as though towards greater light,
towards whatever else I might have done but didn't.

Whatever Else I Might Have Done But Didn't

I have managed to not do harm (unless
mosquitos count, and ants when they appear
next to the canisters on my white
counter, black grains of them smaller
than rice, vaporized under the sponge
with my hand on it, and the centipede
I once found in the leg of my jeans
and the snake I mistook for a rattler
stretched across my doorway—I went
for the bladed shovel—and that
I do regret, with what has become
a residual ache of the stab, the torrent,
the *what have I done* that doubled me over)—

I *have* done harm. And now
I recall my repeated failures to walk
in the shoes of someone who
hurt me or pissed me off or lied to me.
Failures to praise, failures to listen,
failures to get in a bully's face.
Failures to pick up the phone
in a spirit of welcome. Failures to meet
the eyes of a panhandler at an intersection
even as I noted the hard beauty
of bone beneath his weathered cheek.

What will my face reveal about me
when I'm too old to rearrange it,
when I've really forgotten, when I am
no longer at my own mercy—what little of it
I tended? What shape will mercy take
then, and where will it come from?

I have done harm. It has gone around
and come around, but sometimes

it rearranged itself into lessons I could
read. In the reading, I let myself
double over and be flooded. Speared
and washed clean. In the reading, at least
for those moments, I was harmless.

Harmless:

Most animals in populated areas
of Europe and the U.S.
Most animals who live with humans.
All animals while drinking water.
Animals while asleep.

I mean *without guile.*
Dwelling in a singularity
of focus, a state natural to them
and rare in humans. Harmless
to humans, in whom singular focus

is hard-won unless they're threatened
or hunting. Animals harm animals they hunt
but rarely hunt humans unless humans
threaten them, though in swamps
and sea water, all bets are off—

consider alligators, water moccasins, sharks,
jellyfish, lampreys flashing a single tooth,
the giant squid, the Monster of Loch Ness,
the piranha, the killer whale who wouldn't
have killed humans if humans hadn't

corralled it and broken its heart—humans
don't belong in water anyway, not
any more, their former dominion over it
several million years expired. Some animals
who thrive in water remain uncontested, cold-

blooded and totally *other,* sustaining multiple
traditions of cautionary tales, revered and feared
by those who speak and sing, grow hair, bear

burdens of memory, nurse their young,
know how to smile, and walk on two legs

that are neither swift nor strong.

Neither Swift Nor Strong

Today sunflowers have reappeared
along the Rim Road, small wild ones
waving like coins. Soon chamisa will butter
the grassy banks, and then aspen trace their
networks of flame—so the familiar progression
resumes, the nights growing crisp, each plant
preparing to flare with plumage before signing off.

Jogging to forestall the subtractions time
wants to make from my body, I stop
to chat with Donna, earth-woman with thick
silver hair and bad hips, midwife to exuberant
poppies, lilies, daisies and succulents
barely contained by their fence. She zeroes in
on what I don't know I've been afraid of

and gives it the feeling of a name. I don't have
words for it yet, but some of the words she uses,
laughing from the belly, are *impermanence,
who knows?* and *fuck it.* Loss does not spill from her
hands or bow her shoulders. She must think me unfinished,
shuffling doggedly every day past her garden, its celebrations
soon to subside, as though I alone might be spared.

Being Spared

takes hard work—bellows
on spent embers, flare of ambition,
inspiration with nowhere to go—
why not sit awhile and be
a rock in a stream or gale? Buffed
to a shine. Not pushing back. A break
from the perfect lawn. The flurry of attention.
The demands of getting what one
thought one wanted.

The Demands Of Getting What One Thinks One Wants

make me want to get up from the desk
and inspect the refrigerator—this, after
salmon, wild rice, and chocolate. The old
hollow. Perhaps a bit of goat Gouda
would help—after all, the French,
whose language also fills me with hunger,
end each layered meal with cheese.... Once
you start courting the world, you're stuck
with having to dress up even in private, sipping
offered spirits and remembering the manners you
spurned in your prolonged adolescence as you write
thank-you notes on-line and ask, please ...while the day
slips away. Slips into the night full of scents
and rustlings outside the screened door, something
delicious to the cats you want to protect
from owls and coyotes by keeping them inside.
They see into the darkness and know what it
offers. They won't tell you. They could
lose themselves in it.

In It

Once at a retreat, all of us forbidden
speech for a day, I found myself
translating the breezes off the Pacific—
their many registers of hush
through palm and banana leaves—
and tracing endlessly the flight loops
of frigate birds, great wings hardly moving,
their dense bodies lifted on the heft of thermals.

All day I felt a lightness
widening in my chest, its membrane
pressed but not broken by the habit
taken out of reach, the impulse
I had lived by. And my eyes—
I felt them deepen, washed bluer,
pouring over the others a calmness

so strange to me
even as I drew each of them in
along with the sun that sifted through
our hair and thin shirts, and the dusk
that settled around each face
as we ate dinner outdoors, cushioned
in our deep privacies—I could have drifted
forever in that shared restraint

but one man found it too much.
How sadly, then, I returned
to my known self and lost the depths
my eyes had claimed, lost the greening
of my thoughts and lost, until
now, the memory of those
hours without speech.

Without Speech

Once, I made myself
spend a whole night in a field
alone beside a fire. No sleep, no
music, no print. I expected a test, not
a gift. Not a flowing into the play of molten
gold, and smoke rising into a darkness
softened and cleared by everyone else's sleep—
I thought my questions, and the fire answered
in wood almost breaking (*soften your will, don't
relinquish it*) or wood collapsing to embers
(*honor what has ended, and wait*) or one
log glowing among the others, almost
transparent, holding its shape (*you're
on track, stay the course*), the night all metaphor
and spark, embers passing light
among themselves in a flow of collapse
and rebirth. Smoke settled on my jacket and hair
like a benediction. The messages subsided
to something rhythmic, liquid, light
moving in waves through wood, then coals,
then cresting to licks of gold when more wood
took hold. A grief I didn't know I'd harbored
flared, then thinned to ash and drifted off.
Another grief. And another.
The hours wrapped themselves around
what was left of me, something transparent
whose shape I could feel, almost
grasped, for the first time.
Company I could keep.

Company I Can Keep

The sky after last night's rain
has a metallic sheen, layered in thin
clouds that allow morning's rays
to sift through. Today my story un-tells
the likelihood of limelight and brings
instead the smell of pine needles,
fallen and warmed, a mild reassurance,
the smell of Wisconsin summers.
My story. All it ever wanted was to
nudge me into a state of worthiness.
Poor it! Unreliable narrator, lens
that skews the world—my story
lags behind me, easily distracted,
not yet an elder like I am
but ready to shed another layer
of its youth in the mild sun, using nose
instead of need, allowing warm sap
to offer up fragments of other summers
while I sit outdoors reading poems
by an older poet whose work
sustains me, and absorbing the grace, the non-
grasping, the purity of light and frond
through his practiced eyes. Today I can imagine
being even older, walking into the day
accepting each thought without the tic
of apology, near the end of a long
life of work I have done for the love of it.

For The Love Of It

could be enough, ink
loving the nib
and the clean page. Loving
the solitary voice,
trickle of voice that elsewhere
tumbles as a froth
out of control; even in sleep
the tangled brain churns
out dream fragments—they
bob all night, refusing
to quiet, to sink—or else
I wake and stay wakeful
until dawn, unable to
cease listening to whatever it is
that lives in me, arguing with
itself—themselves?—it's tireless—
I can't even be sure
all this commotion comes from
just the brain, grey mess surrounded
by membrane, too small to hold
such a populace, such perplexed
machinery —do *I* harbor it
or does *it* harbor me?—
and to think every person
on this earth carries this…
universe. It can't be measured
or seen or handled. Which is
why, when it narrows through
the nib of a certain pen, I hear
only one voice
teased out of the multitude,
unhurried in its flow
to a destination I can't see but know
waits somewhere. For me.

Waiting Somewhere For Me

is a life I have yet
to face—a life adrift
despite its moorings in work,
soulmates, slash of mountains
behind the house …. When you're well into
the latter half of life and still have one
vigorous parent, when you know how
to step into the elder you have become,
you still can't imagine a life without
that person who has always watched you,
loved you unconditionally

and conditionally (*get your hair out of
your face, are you going to wear THAT?*),
sometimes an adversary, now a weekly
phone call and often guide (*how far apart
should I plant begonias? What's that Italian
aria for tenors that starts like this…?*),
cocktail companion and model for
how to keep seeing the glass half-full
as hips and knees, energy and powers
of concentration fall and rise.

How odd it is to be still a *daughter*—
someone who, in one person's eyes,
is still *becoming*…. I can't imagine
the weightlessness, the free fall
I will be thrust into when she
is no longer there to talk to.
For many years I honed myself, defined
myself, into being not her.

Being Not Her

I did not know how to flirt
or sew or navigate my days, as she did,
without a trace of self-doubt. My demeanor
was serious (*You need to have
a light touch with boys. And remember
to make them feel important*). She
stayed married until death did them part
after 69 years. I married twice and did not
change my name. She adored men. I
was afraid men would distract me. Men
adored her. I wanted them to adore me
and also to leave me alone. I wrote poems
she didn't understand and stopped reading
as our lives deepened into their separate modes.
I resented my native suburb, her comfort zone—
but oh, the lilacs and lily-of-the-valley every
spring, their perfumes thrilling, filling me
with the promise of being grown up, even after
I knew better. Every year I miss them
as I add annuals to my own high-desert square
of decent soil, guided by her words: *don't be afraid
to experiment. You'll remember what thrives.*

What Thrives

Begonias in shade. Primroses
in sun. Lichen anywhere—ditto
thistles, dandelions and crabgrass.

The Clintons in their day. Kennedys
and Roosevelts in their day.

Percussion and trombones in Souza's inner ear.

Gamblers who play for odds rather than winners,
who bet what I've been told is "smart money"
and never need a day job.

Cockroaches in a 4ᵗʰ floor walkup.
Cockroaches in a respectable restaurant kitchen.
Cockroaches in uptown apartments of Columbia professors
whose kids go to private schools…

maybe I'm thinking *persistence*, as in rock
and ridge line and reef. Maybe *thrive* means
to flare and prevail for an age, a generation,
a season, a day and then give way, offering up

its molecules or shoulders to something new
to feed from or stand on.

Something New

suggests a solution to boredom. Boredom in children
is regarded askance by parents and is said to stem
from *lack of inner resources*, as John Berryman
puts it in *Dream Song #14*, his persona—
Henry/Henry Pussycat/ Mr. Bones/himself—
having suffered greatly for lack of them.
But he got two books full of lamentation out of
his/their existential malaise and sexual frustration,
not to mention a Pulitzer—O the trials of lust
and erudition in the educated male....

The inability to overcome boredom is one symptom
of depression, something a surprising number
of celebrities admit to. This is intended
to console the many un-rich and un-famous
who find themselves staring out a pinched window
into grey sky over a sink full of greasy water,
bearing the weight of limited material resources
as in, *How do I choose between keeping*
my water from being shut off, and paying down
my daughter's hospital bills?

The un-famous report these conflicts to researchers
who will go home to appliances that hum
inaudibly, and to track lighting that eases the glare
of what's been in their faces all day. The voices
of the hard-pressed do not sound tremulous over
the microphones. They are not depressed
at those moments, their inner resources having risen
to the occasion. They've stayed in the game by moving
meager funds from Peter to Paul, though the odds
persist in being not in their favor. And then

there are mothers everywhere battling lack of sleep,
lack of help, and hormonal surges. They are the ones

on whose shoulders the new Important Ones
will stand—whose breasts and still-of-night
bottles will feed them, whose packed lunches
and coming-to-the-bedroom-after-nightmares
will back them until they come of age
as conquerors, inventors and healers, agile
and upright, with no memory of those first years of
being watery-limbed, incontinent, and carried.

Watery-limbed, Incontinent, And Carried

looked like no fun to me as a two-year-old
with a new brother. In fact, the state of babyhood
struck me as more boring than the nap
I was made to take each afternoon, my first
experience of the Void, and later an opportunity

to feel my way into rooms of imagination. I yelled
at a cobweb on the ceiling, delighted by the roar
of my voice. My ability to sound enraged. I learned
the power of *pretend*—to reach into a place I
didn't know in order to tell myself a new

story—all of this, to keep from being anything
like that fat, passive creature who, as far
as I could tell, had no life whatsoever.
Perhaps I have pitted a share of my life against
such helplessness. It has chafed me into lacing up

my Nikes to head out in any weather, maybe to resurrect
that first room with its pale walls and single cobweb.
When I run, I feel something like wind shifting inside me.
When I come back in to think, something invisible
sits down too. Something that loves me.

Something That Loves Me

prompts me to press fresh dirt firmly
but not *too* firmly around the transplanted
primroses and lavender, because it
loves them too. And brings mild rain
right after, ensuring the soil will replicate
hothouse perfection during their first night
in an imperfect garden; so the new plantings
look happy at sundown, covered in droplets
and released from the pots that forced them
skyward. With luck they'll spread a little,
then sleep all winter and in May spring up
twice their present size—every year, more
survivors greet me after the final frost and thaw,
having surrendered mass and all their green
to the shortened days of snow and weak light
yet multiplying, in secret, their leaf clusters
and purple sunbursts. So something that loves me
works underground, loving what persists
and does no harm, loving all of us who do one
gentle thing and then get out of the way.

Gentle Things That Get Out Of The Way:

A whisper close to a single ear in the crowd;
hand's touch that barely parts the air
and might be mistaken for breeze; a smile
behind a veil; a smile that lights briefly in one
set of eyes like a firefly set free in the dark;
garden scents that stir memory and withdraw
(or were they imagined?), leaving one
bemused in the skin of a former self; patch of
sun brushing fur; patch of sun moving on
while the window holds the world in place;
the tide leaving gifts in the sand for egrets to find;
fog bringing the lights on, then rolling back to sea.

At Sea

Sea lions near the Embarcadero
duplicate themselves in the sun, on docks
reserved for them by environmentalists, though
this is prime real estate for boats at the white-capped
midpoint of San Francisco Bay. They drape themselves
over one another like kittens in a too-small basket, sleek
and nearly half a ton each, sleek, basking on weathered boards
once set up to berth yachts owned by a species
higher on the food chain. Most seem content
to use each other for pillows, though at times
there's a small skirmish over territory—a bark,
a small mouth opening (more whiskers than teeth),
flail of muscled neck—clearly their language of hierarchy
is more nuanced than a brandishing of arms. Their eyes
are dark pools, their snouts blunted to gentleness—what
might it be like to run a hand along the onyx-and-intelligent
muscle of one? To fall in with what is evidently real
conversation? I lie in the berth of a small boat, this marina
our motel, and listen to their gutturals on turf they've
claimed, though they seem no longer to be quarrelling—
no crescendos or pauses, more an ongoing succession
of spondees. The tourists, like us, have left them to their
late-night—what? Courtship? Philosophical musings?
Soon I will fall asleep in this rough comma of bay
dreaming, perhaps, I can parse what they're saying
and say something back they might hear as like-minded.

Like-minded

Domesticated dogs, ever willing to please,
would have us think they think like us—
they are princely in their concession to our need
to be The Center of Everything—each panting snout
looks like a smile as a canine face gazes up
at its human.... I myself am guilty of thinking
I'm loved by any animal I find loveable, which translates:
if I dissolve before your paw raised towards me, or your
sentient whiskers brushing my palm, or your goofy
lopsided ears, you must be drawn equally to me by the force
of my brimming tenderness. I've never hugged
a tree, but I could err in the presence of a furred creature
that may fear me or want to kill me—its beauty. Its
otherness. Its smallness. Its largeness. Its athleticism
in its element, be that air or water, tree or tunnel.
Blindness and longing—I can't slip from ignorance
that binds me, this net of being human.

This Net Of Being Human

is a condition I don't want to disparage
though plenty do, picking over the guilt of being
too much, not enough, the only species
that does terrible things on purpose
to the earth and each other.... I still pry myself
from warm sheets every morning and put
one foot into a slipper. The other into another.
And rise on legs that hold me upright
as they were designed to do. Wash face.
Insert drops that soothe my eyes
to readiness to look at the world again.

Start the coffee, warm the cup—my ritual
for revving the little engines in my head
and somewhere else—the heart? I may stall
over an advertisement flung through cyberspace,
a request from someone who just wants to be heard
and bits of throwaway news. But eventually a half-
formed *something* stirs and gathers itself
into a thought, no one asking, no one
waiting to praise. Then another. So I move
into the one day. On my two legs. In my one heart.

In My One Heart

I have lived as two people,
one more fearless than the other.
One who prefers to stay at home
then is the last to leave a party.
One mostly helpless. One
myopic. One with a green thumb.
One who every morning burns the bacon.

Both have trouble getting caps off jars.
One can hold a sulk with practiced
tenacity. One can mimic any sound
a cat makes, though she doesn't understand
what's been said. One prefers black.
One experiments, lately, with coral.

One has taught herself to like cheap scotch.
One prefers any wine whose description includes
the word "velvet." One has never married.
One has married four times.
One likes men. The other likes men.
One likes them one at a time and far between.

One has never mastered eyeliner.
One says she can't paint and won't try.
One can paint because she doesn't care
and because making a mess is liberating
as long as it's not on her face. One is good at
finding small objects on the ground—she

is not the myopic one. The one who
burns bacon may be the one whose perennials
come back every spring. The one who likes black
has been known to wear turquoise. It has become
hard to determine who is who, and in fact

there may be more than two; one heart evidently is not large enough to give everyone a room of her own.

Her. Own.

Owning—this is hard for women
of a certain generation—mine—
or maybe it's just the Apology Gene
women of all ages have, hidden or not.
I watch myself *dis*own, on autopilot,
as though I might ward off censure by
censuring myself first. Smoothing in advance
the waves my voice might make. Maybe I need
a bark collar that zings a soft spot every time
I demur and start to shrink-wrap some
part of my self—not a jolt, just a subtle
reminder that I'm doing something more
painful, and painful for a longer time,
than anything a bit of voltage can do.

How would it feel to move through the world
without this ploy at self-protection? As, say,
a first-born son or a drill sergeant
or an English don? To assert a position
or give an order as though it were
expected? I can barely imagine being able to
disguise uncertainty, waiting it out, though I can
guess that has its own way of being no fun....
Perhaps the male counterpart to my collar
would prompt a man to open an interchange
with a question. Or speculation. *Get over it*, I say and say
to myself, chewing over this bone well into the night
while the lovely man I am cleaved to puts up with my
leaving all the lights on after he has gone to bed.

Gone To Bed

Gone fishing.
Gone dreaming.
Gone where dreams
take us to what a psychic
once told me is a parallel universe
as real as the place we fell asleep in,
its cityscapes, missed planes, lost luggage,
jump-cuts and inexplicable behaviors
continuing to manifest and shape-shift long
after we wake up and forget them. That might
explain how an aftertaste, whiff of presence, essence
of someone I've never met but somehow know
surfaces now and then—a brief, gossamer visitation—
as though bleeding through the gauze that is my life,
the gauze that may be a dream someone else is having.

Someone Is Having

a meltdown across the canal
behind one of the balcony railings
I can see from our cockpit. The someone
is probably no more than three.
The apartments overlook the marina
we berth in, a no-nonsense facility
that nevertheless holds a few yachts that
cost more than a second home
alongside modest sailboats like ours.
The apartments are, I'm told, low-income
housing frequented by people whose English
is still in its nascent stages, apartments
that are all narrow angles and half-hearted windows
despite their proximity to water and a view
of people like us. The someone having a meltdown
is trying mightily to learn a language that will
thrust her into a new world and help her stay there.
Help her channel whatever wants to be released
at the moment—the weight of what the parents
haven't figured out, the weight of her newness
and of what she may remember, for a while,
of the world she arrived from. Of course
I can't know, but her cries contain such depth,
such *direction*—they hold a furious wisdom
if I listen for it—I want no one to hush her.

No One To Hush Her

No one to shame her. No one
to stitch and trim what she feels
into what she should feel, or tamper
with the conduits between what she feels

and what she lets full-voice into the world
as she starts a life without words
and then learns to say them. Then
to read them. Then to write them.

And later, no one to tell her too brutally
she's not ironic enough, not edgy, not urban,
not male, not rigorous, not subtle
though of course for a long time she is

none of these things—how can she be
if she's to take in enough of her surroundings
to try on as much as she can while she is still
in a state of *becoming?* And who's to say

how long that should take? Or that it shouldn't
continue in waves, between bouts of having
become? And who's to say this is not
a hero's journey?—not the old coming-out-of-

trauma tale, not a wrestling with shame,
but a *she* seeking simply to reach beyond
limits that are, for a time, necessary. Not
wounds, but a calling. A rigorous gift.

A Rigorous Gift

A gift of gold, of chocolate, of
something cashed in at the right time
is easily received. But some gifts
bring an asking. Not from
the giver, but from within—

an itch, an impulse
towards the paintbrush,
the blank page, the bat, the barre,
the clay, the torch, the breath, the bow,
the blackboard full of equations

and the waiting. Whole days spent
in a shifting, particulate silence.
One can grow old without knowing
one is growing old, suspended like this
between action and uncertainty.

Uncertainty

A child comes into the world
squinting in the glare and knife-edge
of air, piercing the new element
with cries that are all *I, I, I.* Then settles
into a second self and stays there
for years, hidden, learning to
keep up appearances, or pretending to,
that first flame all but extinguished.
The parents watch anxiously when words
come late, when bedtime paralyzes the spirit
in a bewildering solitude, when baby fat
lingers and hides what the face
will become, when school is the place
where one can't yet hit a ball, or pronounce
r, or read block letters, or meet
the eyes of other children. The parents
have forgotten their own unfolding—
the privacy, the wonder, the loneliness
and germination. So the child begins
the remembered life of *not-know-
how-ness, not-enough-ness, not-in-
time-ness*, though something re-kindles
in secret through the ugly-duckling years
of sulks and missed homework, acne
and lack of charm. Eventually, inexplicably,
the child emerges into possession of poise
and a bank account, a sense of humor
and a significant other. The parents are proud
and full of thanks, everything in balance at last.
For a second time the children, now launched,
jettison a former stage of themselves.
And have children of their own.

Own

Do we, really, *own*
who we once were? Own
up?—if so, own up to *what?*
The fact that we viewed our
child selves reductively, mistaking
the chip for the whole shoulder?
I do remember a shrinking child,
fearful spirit who found herself ill-
suited to the world she was born to—
that forced grin in family photos, hair
crazed with electricity, fear of cap guns,
inexplicable attraction to a single garnet
shaped like a teardrop, aversion
to slugs and scrambled eggs…. *Stop.*
We all start out as eccentrics. Isn't that
amazing? *Own* is close to *owe.* I say
to that child, *You are everything. I've become.*

Everything. I've Become.

Is Facebook replacing the real face?
Is Google making us lazy? Is YouTube
devouring an entire culture's discretionary time?
Research reveals the contemporary self is obsessed
with fame, the famous, and animal videos.
Can't sustain an average wait of more than
15.3 seconds before receiving an answer. Craves
visibility. Fears anonymity more than bankruptcy,
divorce, and kidney stones....

The Benedictine practice of *Lectio Divina,* dating
from the 6ᵗʰ century, was conceived to help seekers
access the peace of the Divine
rather than pin down the Divine:
Leggere. Read slowly.
Meditare. Meditate on what you have read.
Pregare. Respond to text.
Contemplare. Allow the self to empty in the presence of text...

as on *paper.* The weight of it. The residual
wood of it. And a pen underlining
a you-shaped space that fills with not-you.
Six miles high, on the plane, no one
knows this rootless you. No one tweets
in your direction. You peer into
text—a single act of thought unspooling—
and grow lighter than air.

Lighter Than Air

I came into the world as a fist
of cells, a pebble, aware of its weight
even as it floated in a night sea.
And part of me remains

in the dark, astonished by the life
I find myself in—its cities, its lights,
swift travel, love, lies, heated rooms
and soft places to sleep—where
was I before?

I watched my father relinquish, in his
ninety-sixth year, whatever had
anchored him to this world—the woods,
the smell of motor oil, lake water,
tools, the remembered taste
of tobacco—leaving the weight of
what he would be after fire changed bone
to something like sand, and the rest
had moved somewhere else.

Somewhere Else.

I think I've been a boulder in other lives.
Harder to move than I am in this one.
Perhaps I'll be finer in my next—
at times I can almost silence the goings-on
in my head, noise of here-and-now,
a granular frequency that may not be all
but is mostly what I hear.

I would like to know what my father
saw while I sat beside him
and breath and warmth left his body
imperceptibly, with surprising gentleness
as though a feather had passed over us both.
I would like to know if it changed me too

but for now I remain a handful of something hard
thrown against glass. Someday ash, most
of which will sink into the soil it came from
and a trace of which may float, if I keep
asking, into mist, then air, then
something thinner.

About Leslie Ullman

Leslie Ullman is the author of four poetry collections, most recently *Progress on the Subject of Immensity* (University of New Mexico Press, 2013. Her first collection, *Natural Histories*, won the Yale Series of Younger Poets Prize, and *Slow Work Through Sand* won the Iowa Poetry Prize. She has published a hybrid book of craft essays and writing exercises, *Library of Small Happiness* (3: A Taos Press, 2017). She is Professor Emerita at University of Texas-El Paso and teaches in the low-residency MFA Program at Vermont College of the Fine Arts. Now a resident of Taos, New Mexico, she teaches skiing in the winters at Taos Ski Valley.

Acknowledgements

I am grateful to the following publications in which some of these poems first appeared:

Poet Lore, under slightly different titles:
Time, Tasted
Waste?

Bordersenses:
God's Eye, a Spiral

The Heart's Many Doors: American Poets Respond to Metka Krasovec's Images Responding to Emily Dickenson:
Folded in on Itself
The Noticing
Gentle Things That Get Out of the Way
The You that All Along Has Housed You
For a Time I Believe I Can Touch Them
Not Holding Back
A Rigorous Gift

Journal of Feminist Studies in Religion:
Lighter Than Air
Next Time Around